NOT LIKE ME

First published in 2025 by OH
An Imprint of HEADLINE PUBLISHING GROUP LIMITED

1

Disclaimer:
This book has not been licensed, approved, sponsored, or endorsed by Kendrick Lamar

Kendrick Lamar is a registered trademark owned by Nomo Hashimoto LLC.

Cataloguing in Publication Data is available from the British Library

ISBN 978-1-03543-648-4

Compiled and written by: Malcolm Croft
Editorial: Matt Tomlinson
Designed and typeset in Avenir by: Andy Jones
Project manager: Russell Porter
Production: Arlene Lestrade
Printed and bound in Dubai

Headline's policy is to use papers that are natural, renewable and recyclable products and made from wood grown in well-managed forests and other controlled sources. The logging and manufacturing processes are expected to conform to the environmental regulations of the country of origin.

HEADLINE PUBLISHING GROUP LIMITED
An Hachette UK Company
Carmelite House, 50 Victoria Embankment, London EC4Y 0DZ

The authorised representative in the EEA is Hachette Ireland, 8 Castlecourt Centre, Dublin 15, D15 XTP3, Ireland (email: info@hbgi.ie)

www.headline.co.uk   www.hachette.co.uk

NOT LIKE ME

THE LITTLE GUIDE TO KENDRICK LAMAR

UNOFFICIAL AND UNAUTHORIZED

CONTENTS

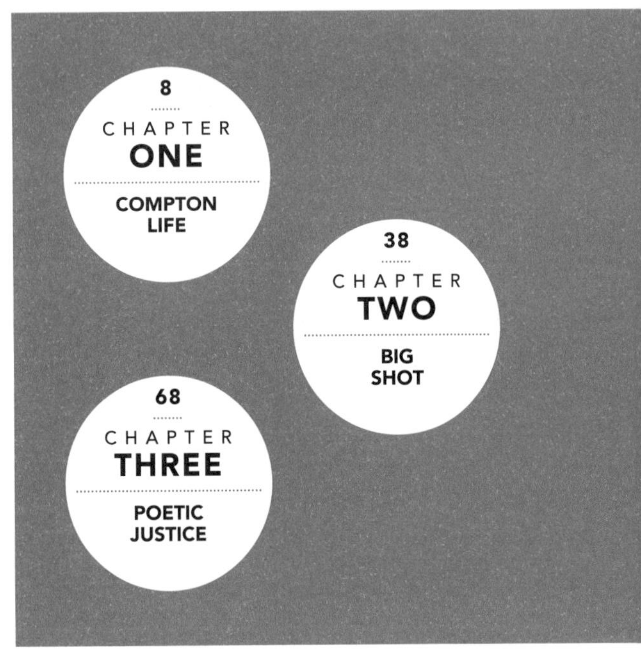

INTRODUCTION

In the two decades since his first arrival on the West Coast rap scene, Kendrick Lamar has evolved from a troubled Compton kid stuttering on the street corner to a creative genius responsible for breaking down major cultural barriers. Along the way he has earned a feast of inspiring titles, from the "voice of a generation" to "Hood Beethoven", "Pulitzer Kenny" to the "poet laureate of hip-hop" – all of which highlight just how highly influential and important he has become. To put it simply, Kendrick is the undisputed GOAT.

Fearless, innovative, philosophical... Kendrick Lamar is a storyteller who unites all of these elements with style and substance into a career that has not only defined his generation but defied it too. To him, his role as the "greatest rapper alive" is more than just a responsibility, it's a calling – he is on a mission from God to enlighten the world one verse at a time. It's clearly working.

A Pulitzer Prize-winning, multi-million-selling, culture-reckoning force of nature, and an artist who regularly breaks the Internet with a killer turn of phrase, Kendrick has redefined what rap and hip-hop can be in a masterful blend of soaring, searing, sermons with pinpoint social commentary all set to earthquake-sized beats that can't help but shake your feet. Put simply: he's not like us.

After all, how many other artists can make global headlines for their beef with another hip-hop superstar – then go on to perform the iconic diss track on the biggest stage in the world: the Super Bowl.

This Little Guide to Kendrick Lamar is loaded with the rapper's signature wit, wisdom and wicked way with words, a tiny tome that makes for an ideal introduction to the iconic artist, as well as the perfect present for long-time, loyal fans. He has millions of both, trust us. Enjoy!

CHAPTER ONE

COMPTON LIFE

Kendrick Lamar's origin story is filled with riots and lootings, gangbanging and drive-by shootings, as he survived hood life in Los Angeles's most notorious badland: Compton.

A straight-A student at Centennial High School in Compton, LA (the same school as future mentor Dr. Dre), Kendrick was always a unique unknown to his peers, a softly-spoken deep thinker – and a gang all to himself...

My father is a complete realist. My mother is the dreamer. That's my DNA – the yin and the yang. It starts there first, before I even heard any type of melody or lyric.

Kendrick, on what makes him he who he is, interview with Rick Rubin, *GQ*, October 20, 2016.

My mom and my pops were influential. They played everything to me – Gangsta rap to oldies. You'd hear Snoop, Dre and then you'd hear Marvin Gaye on the next track. I'd stay in my corner, listening, and eventually they'd say, 'What you've got to do in life is find something positive.'

Kendrick, on the powerful influence of his mother and father, interview with Sryon, *HipHopDX*, August 28, 2012.

One day, my pops told me: 'A man is one who sticks to what he has decided, not what others have decided for him. Be your own gang.'

Kendrick, on his father's advice about gang life in Compton, LA, interview with Stéphanie Binet, *Le Monde*, March 15, 2025.

"

My pops, he was tough. He was militant. He never showed no weakness. He never showed any emotion that could garner a one-up from the person sitting across from him. I experienced that not knowing I had them same traits.

"

Kendrick, on his childhood and his relationship with his father, Interview with SZA, *Harpers' Bazaar*, October 21, 2024.

> “99 per cent of my music is specific events.”

Kendrick, on the autobiographical quality of his lyrical subject matter, interview with Dorian Lynskey, *The Guardian*, June 21, 2015.

Kendrick's surname, Lamar, is actually his middle name. He was born Kendrick Lamar Duckworth – hence his first stage name, K.Dot – on June 17, 1987, in Compton, Los Angeles.

The rapper's mother, Paula, gave him the name Kendrick after the singer Eddie Kendricks from iconic Motown group, The Temptations. His father, Kenny, approved.

On the day I was born, my pops was playing Big Daddy Kane when I actually came from the hospital. He was blasting the music and my mom's cussing his ass out all the way to Compton!

Kendrick, on his father's deep love of hip-hop music, interview with Zack O'Malley Greenburg, *Forbes*, November 14, 2017.

To date, Kendrick has released six highly influential studio albums.

His biggest-selling album so far was *DAMN.*, which was the seventh biggest album of 2017 and sold more than four million copies worldwide.

1. ***Section.80*** (2011)
2. ***Good Kid, M.A.A.D City*** (2012)
3. ***To Pimp a Butterfly*** (2015)
4. ***DAMN.*** (2017)
5. ***Mr. Morale & the Big Steppers*** (2022)
6. ***GNX*** (2024)

Which is your favourite?

In Chicago, my mom told my dad, 'I can't fuck with you if you ain't trying to better yourself. We can't be in the streets forever.' They were going to move to San Bernardino, but my auntie Tina was in Compton. She got 'em a hotel until they got on their feet, and my mom got a job at McDonald's. For the first couple of years they slept in their car or motels, or in the park when it was hot enough. Eventually, they saved enough money to get their first apartment, and that's when they had me.

Kendrick, on his parents' earliest movements, from their gang-affiliated troubles in Chicago to their move to Compton in 1984, believing it would be safer, interview with Marcus J. Moore, *The Nation*, October 8, 2020.

As a teenager, the majority of my interactions with police were… not good. There were a few good cops who were actually protecting the community. But then you have ones from the Valley. They never met me in their life, but since I'm a kid in basketball shorts and a white T-shirt, they want to slam me on the hood of the car. Sixteen years old. Even if someone's not a good kid, that don't give them the right to slam a minor on the ground, or pull a pistol on him.

”

Kendrick, on being a victim of police brutality and racial profiling as a kid, interview with Marcus J. Moore, *The Nation*, October 8, 2020.

My parents were fairly young in Compton. They were the hip crowd. So I was exposed to all these new artists, from Big Daddy Kane to Eazy-E to the Bay Area – Too Short, E-40 – to Marvin Gaye and the Isley Brothers. Their field of music just broadened my ideas to come. But I never would've thought in a million years that I'd be doing it.

”

Kendrick, on icons and influences as his inspiration, interview with Lisa Robinson, *Vanity Fair*, June 28, 2018.

Nothing is ever sugar-coated in Compton. You wake up every morning and pray to God that you see another.

Kendrick, on his childhood in Compton, interview with Sryon, *HipHopDX*, August 28, 2012.

A guy was out there serving his narcotics and somebody rolled up with a shotgun and blew his chest out. It did something to me right then and there. It let me know that this is not only something that I'm looking at, but it's something that maybe I have to get used to.

”

Kendrick, on witnessing his first drive-by murder aged five, interview with Marcus J. Moore, *The Nation*, October 8, 2020.

Eight years old, walking home from McNair Elementary. Dude was in the drive-thru ordering his food, and homey ran up, boom boom – smoked him. After that, I just got numb to it.

Kendrick, on witnessing his second drive-by murder, aged eight, interview with Marcus J. Moore, *The Nation*, October 8, 2020.

I've seen my own blood shed – and I've been the cause of other people shedding their blood.

Kendrick, on his gang-affiliated childhood in Compton, interview with Lisa Robinson, *Vanity Fair*, June 28, 2018.

We was broke, but we wasn't broken.

Kendrick, on his childhood and close-knit family upbringing, interview with Lisa Robinson, *Vanity Fair*, June 28, 2018.

I would wake up one morning, and it would be cartoons and cereal and school. And at 4 p.m., we'd be having a house party 'til 11 p.m. And then people were shooting each other outside the door. That was my lifestyle. And it's not only mine; it's so many other individuals'. And I wanted to tell that story.

Kendrick, on his Compton childhood as his earliest songwriting inspiration, interview with Lisa Robinson, *Vanity Fair*, June 28, 2018.

"

I don't know if somebody threw a rocket at a trash can or what, but it made a loud-ass popping sound and everybody who was in the car with me ducked. The instinct to get out the way when you hear a popping sound, that's real for me. I'm sure it's real for a lot of artists who grew up in neighbourhoods like Compton.

"

Kendrick, on the frequency of drive-by shootings in Compton during his childhood, interview with Dorian Lynskey, *The Guardian*, June 21, 2015.

As a kid from Compton, you can get all the success in the world and still question your worth.

”

Kendrick, on his self-worth, interview with Marcus J. Moore, *The Nation*, October 8, 2020.

My father said, 'I don't want you to be like me.' He said, 'I never want you to make the mistakes I made. You can't wind up out on the corner.' He knew by the company I kept what I was gettin' into. Out of respect for him, I gathered myself together.

Kendrick, on his father's advice to aspire to be more than just in a gang, interview with Marcus J. Moore, *The Nation*, October 8, 2020

It doesn't matter if I say I love my community and that I love Black people. It means nothing if when I run into an enemy from 10 years ago all I want to do is get back at him for what he did to my homies. Suddenly, all the statements about Black pride go out the window. Whether I like it or not, it's in me. All it takes is one bad phone call to send me back there.

Kendrick, on retribution, interview with Stéphanie Binet, *Le Monde*, March 15, 2025.

I grew up in a Black and Mexican world. I don't recall ever seeing a white person, whether it was a student or a teacher, in all my years of school. I got used to that, so it's a culture shock when I met all these different cultures and ethnicities.

Kendrick, on leaving Compton for the first time, interview with Insanula Ahmed, *Complex*, July 25, 2014.

After one of my homeboys got smoked, a friend's grandmother had seen that we weren't right in the head. She told us to find God. That was her being an angel for us. I took it to the next level – underwater. I felt like it was something I had to do, just for that reassurance and belief in God.

”

Kendrick, on his first of two baptisms, one at age 16 and again in his 20s, after a friend's grandmother was worried that his gangbanging was going to get him killed, interview with Joe Coscarelli, *New York Times*, March 16, 2015.

“

My story? I was a good kid in a mad city.

”

Kendrick, on his story, interview with Zack O'Malley Greenburg, *Forbes*, November 14, 2017.

> "I know where I come from. I know the hurt that I've caused families. Those are my demons."

Kendrick, on his formative years gangbanging in Compton, interview with Joe Coscarelli, *New York Times*, March 16, 2015.

I fell in love with hip-hop at four years old. My parents played music all day in the house. It's always been my passion. It's more than just music for me – it's a lifestyle.

Kendrick, on his early love of hip-hop music, interview with Zack O'Malley Greenburg, *Forbes*, November 14, 2017.

Whether it's through gang violence, police brutality, drugs or women, it's the circumstances around us that turn us evil. I was exposed to it too, but I was fortunate enough to have an active pops to show me the stepping stones and what was right... and wrong. Most of the friends I grew up with didn't have a pops.

Kendrick, on the importance of having a father growing up, interview with Sryon, *HipHopDX*, June 10, 2011.

“

When you’re from Compton, you grow up quick, but you only know maybe a four-block radius. That’s all the world has to offer.

”

Kendrick, on his formative days “on the street corner” in Compton, LA, interview with Insanula Ahmed, *Complex*, July 25, 2014.

CHAPTER TWO

BIG SHOT

Kendrick's earliest musical successes date back as early as 2003, when the rapper's mixtapes and poetic lyrical prowess – often perfected on street corners – received the praise of Kendrick's friends… and LA record labels, such as Top Dawg Entertainment, who signed Kendrick in 2005 when he was just 17.

Kendrick's first mixtape (released under the name K.Dot), *Youngest Head N*gga in Charge (Hub City Threat: Minor of the Year)*, was released while the young rapper was still in high school!

The 26-track set showed off Kendrick's raw and rare rapping talent and it caught the attention of Anthony Tiffith, CEO of Top Dawg Entertainment, who signed the rapper in 2005.

Over the next few years, Kendrick continued to build his reputation with a series of mixtapes, including *Training Day* (2005), *No Sleep 'Til NYC* (a collaboration with Jay Rock in 2007) and *C4* (2009).

Fame costs you a little bit of everything. The number one thing it costs you is relationships. I can eat, sleep and breathe music, but some people can't really understand that. So they have assumptions to try to explain your success for you. They say that you changed, but really, what I learned is that you don't change... but you do change the people around you.

Kendrick, on the consequences of fame and fortune on friends and family, interview with Insanula Ahmed, *Complex*, July 25, 2014.

I had birthdays, Christmas and holidays, which allowed me to actually be a kid. It gave me the ability to be a dreamer. That's what separated me from all my homeboys. I was always dreaming about doing something else or going somewhere else.

Kendrick, on how the stability of his home life as a kid allowed him opportunities his Compton peers never had, interview with Erykah Badu, *Interview*, April 23, 2013.

“

Top Dawg is an OG. But what separated him from a lot of cats, as far as mentorship when I was 15 years old, was he wasn’t inspiring us to do negative things like some individuals do when they have that power in the streets. It was a different swag. He was wanting to see these young individuals be positive with themselves.

”

Kendrick, on Top Dawg (Anthony Tiffith), the first to sign Kendrick to his label, Top Dawg Entertainment, in 2005, and Kendrick’s first musical mentor, interview with Zack O’Malley Greenburg, *Forbes*, November 14, 2017.

I first started rapping when I was 13. I said then that I wanted to sit down and perfect my craft, so I started studying all the greats.

Kendrick, on the start of his career and his influences, including Tupac, Snoop and Dr. Dre, interview with Sryon, *HipHopDX*, June 10, 2011,

"

Don't talk to me about no fucking Raisin Bran. Wheaties? Stop it. You pick that up in the aisle walking with me and I might be liable to punch you in the face if you were my cousin.

"

Kendrick, on cereal (his biggest food love), interview with David Drake, *Complex*, October 24, 2012.

My first day in the vocal booth, Top [Anthony Tiffith] said, 'Let me see if this is really you.' I was just freestyling, rapping whatever came into my head, sweating for two hours. It was the most important moment of my life.

Kendrick, on his first audition for future record label owner Anthony Tiffith, head of Top Dawg Entertainment, interview with Lisa Robinson, *Vanity Fair*, June 28, 2018.

How you stay sane in this business, and never lose the essence of the music, is to never forget the hip-hop roots you come from. I know my forefathers and the people that laid the groundwork for me to be here. I always keep that in the back of my mind. Never take it for advantage and misuse it. As long as you be who you are but respect what got us here, that's how hip-hop can continue to evolve.

Kendrick, on how to evolve hip-hop for the future, interview with Zack O'Malley Greenburg, *Forbes*, November 14, 2017.

With more than 100 million Spotify listeners a month, Kendrick is the fifth most followed artist on the planet, behind Bruno Mars, the Weeknd, Lady Gaga and Billie Eilish.

To date, he has amassed a crazy 50 billion total streams!

His first track to reach one billion streams was 2024's 'Not Like Us', which received a massive 430 per cent increase in Spotify streams the day after Kendrick's iconic Super Bowl Half Time Show performance.

“

The earliest start of my career was Internet-based. At first I didn’t understand it, because I’m from the ’90s and used to having a physical record, something tangible you can feel in your hand. I want to look through the CD and feel it.

”

Kendrick, on being a child of the 1990s and one of the first rappers to see mainstream success solely on digital media such as streaming, interview with Zack O’Malley Greenburg, *Forbes*, November 14, 2017.

I am the greatest rapper alive – and I got there by listening, studying and throwing thousands of pieces of paper away that were garbage.

Kendrick, on his motivation and dedication to succeed, interview with Lisa Robinson, *Vanity Fair*, June 28, 2018.

I can't make my albums just by producers sending me beats. I have to be in the grit with them. I got to be there on every snare, every 808, every transition, every arrangement. I have to be in the nook of it. I'm there for the whole process.

”

Kendrick, on his dedication to the creative process, interview with Brian Hiatt, *Rolling Stone*, August 9, 2017.

When I look around at my classmates and my friends, they all lived with their grandparents. To have a mother and a father in your household – this showed me immediately that anything is possible. It showed me loyalty.

Kendrick, on having two parents at home (unlike his peers), *Vanity Fair*, June 28, 2018.

To Pimp A Butterfly is really about me trying to balance two worlds – where I used to be and where I am today. It was therapy for me. I was looking at myself in the mirror and trying to figure out who I really am.

”

Kendrick, on the duality of 2015's *To Pimp A Butterfly*, interview with Dorian Lynskey, *The Guardian*, June 21, 2015.

Whether I'm at the Grammys or the White House, I can't change where I come from or who I care about.

”

Kendrick, on refusing to change from fortune and fame, interview with Joe Coscarelli, *New York Times*, March 16, 2015.

The name change from K.Dot was me developing myself. I want people to know who I am as a person and what I represent. So I woke up one morning and said, 'The best way to start is to give them me... my real name.'

Kendrick, on reverting his original stage name, K.Dot, back to his birth name in 2009, interview with Sryon, *HipHopDX*, June 10, 2011

I've been stomped in the back. I've been snatched out of cars and had rifles pointed at me. I know our history. Black and brown pride have been taught in my household for a long time.

Kendrick, on police brutality, racial profiling and political disenfranchisement, interview with Joe Coscarelli, *New York Times*, March 16, 2015.

Being invited to the White House wasn't about a kid from Compton going to the White House, it was about Barack Obama letting urban kids walk inside that building... and giving people from a certain community the opportunity to sit down inside that house and have conversations that matter.

”

Kendrick, on President Obama's invitation to Kendrick to visit the White House in 2016, interview with Zack O'Malley Greenburg, *Forbes*, November 14, 2017.

I always thought money was something just to make me happy. But I've learned that I feel better being able to help my folks, because we never had nothing. So, just to see them excited about my career is more of a blessing than me actually having it for myself.

Kendrick, on money and being able to help his parents, interview with Erykah Badu, *Interview*, April 23, 2013.

"Make it sound purple. Make it sound light green."

Kendrick, on his sound-to-colour synaesthesia, a neurological condition that allows him to see music in particular colours, interview with Marcus J. Moore, *The Nation*, October 8, 2020.

Obama reached out! Going to the White House took me back to talking to my grandma, when she was alive, and her telling me what it would be like if we had a black president. The idea gave her hope.

Kendrick, on being invited to President Obama's White House in 2016 to perform for Fourth of July celebrations, interview with Lisa Robinson, *Vanity Fair*, June 28, 2018.

In 2011, onstage, Dr. Dre passed me the torch, and a burst of energy just came out and I had to let it flow. My tears are all on the internet. I love that that happened. It showed me in real time expressing myself and seeing all the work that I put forth actually come to life in that moment.

Kendrick, on the 2011 concert in LA when Snoop Dogg,* Kurupt, Warren G, The Game, and Daz handed the West Coast rap torch to Kendrick Lamar, interview with SZA, *Harper's Bazaar*, October 21, 2024

*After passing Kendrick the torch, Snoop told Kendrick: "You better run with it."

To me, *To Pimp A Butterfly* is perfect for right now. If the world was happy, maybe we'd give you a happy album. But right now, we are not happy.

Kendrick, on the lyrical themes to 2015's To Pimp A Butterfly, interview with Marcus J. Moore, *The Nation*, October 8, 2020.

“

I was inside Dr. Dre’s house one time, and I was like, ‘Damn, this is a big ass house!’ He was like, ‘Yes, it’s a big ass house. The easy part is not getting it... You have to keep this big motherfucker. You got to continue to work’. That stayed with me.

”

Kendrick, on his prolific work ethic, interview with Zack O’Malley Greenburg, *Forbes*, November 14, 2017.

When I changed my name [from K.Dot] to my actual real name, Kendrick Lamar, and found my true story, that's when I started getting the looks and the ears that I wanted.

”

Kendrick, on reverting his stage name [of K.Dot, from 2003–2009] back to his real name, interview with Zack O'Malley Greenburg, *Forbes*, November 14, 2017.

“

This industry will drive you fucking crazy, so I like to sit in a room full of silence. There will be times where I just go to the studio and kick everybody out and just play instrumentals for the whole night because I need that peace of mind – whether it’s 10 minutes, 30 minutes, an hour, four sessions, a day, two weeks. That’s how I relieve stress.

”

Kendrick, on beating stress, interview with Insanula Ahmed, *Complex*, July 25, 2014.

We Love Kendrick Lamar

Kendrick has picked up praise* from countless celebrity admirers over the years…

"He's the Miles Davis of our time, but he's his own thing. His ability to entertain while educating, without ever being preachy, is amazing."

Pharrell Williams

"I can literally listen to his music and become a kid growing up with all the struggles in the inner city, but at the same time learn all the lessons it taught that we use as men today."

LeBron James

"By the end of listening to his first album, I felt like I knew everything about him. He brings you into his world with his lyrics in a way that really paints a clear picture."

Eminem

"For a gentle dude, he throws a righteous punch; I wouldn't get in the way of it."

Bono

"Watching Kendrick Lamar create and record his verses on the 'Bad Blood' remix was one of the most inspiring experiences of my life."

Taylor Swift

"For him to be that naturally talented already and still want to be better is weird, inspiring and beautiful."

SZA

"You just knew this guy was destined for greatness."

Dr. Dre

"Kendrick is one of the best of all time. He exists on another plane."

Rick Rubin

*All quoted in *Vanity Fair*, June 28, 2018

CHAPTER THREE

POETIC JUSTICE

Kendrick's wit and wisdom, and wicked way with words in his rhymes, are as powerful and precise as they are poetic.

The Pulitzer Prize agreed: in 2018, he became the first ever rapper to win the prestigious honour, proof (were it needed) of his game-changing talent.

This is his love of his craft, in his own words....

I've put in well over 10,000 hours of just rappin'. I can rap all day, and freestyle all day. But I said to myself... 'What will separate myself from the other artists out there?'

Kendrick, on what makes him distinct, interview with Zack O'Malley Greenburg, *Forbes*, November 14, 2017.

“

DMX’s *It’s Dark and Hell is Hot* (1998) – that’s the first album that got me into writing. I wrote my first lyrics to that album actually, about 13 or 14. I was in eighth grade. I just got inspired and I started writing. That album inspired me to become a rapper.

”

Kendrick, on his most influential inspiration, interview with David Drake, *Complex*, October 24, 2012.

I didn't read a lot of books growing up – I read the dictionary.

Kendrick, on his literary influences, interview with Lisa Robinson, *Vanity Fair*, June 28, 2018.

In 2017 Kendrick released his fourth studio album *DAMN.* – it went straight to No. 1 in America, his third consecutive No. 1 album.

Praised universally, the politically charged and socially conscious record earned Kendrick the Pulitzer Prize and sold more than four million copies. It also features the culturally significant Black Lives Matter anthem 'Alright'.

The moment I made that decision to get in the studio and actually work and study the culture of hip-hop – and not dabble in everything else that my homeboys was doing – then everything just started to open up and blossom for me.

”

Kendrick, on creation as a means to escape the cycle of Compton violence, interview with Erykah Badu, *Interview*, April 23, 2013.

"The first verse is everything that I feared from the time that I was seven years old. The second verse I was 17, in the third it's everything I feared when I was 27. These verses are completely honest."

Kendrick, on 'Fear', the song he considers his best work, interview with Kiana Fitzgerald, *Complex*, October 16, 2017.

The GOAT Playlist: Kendrick's 10 Tracks

1. **Alright** (2015)
2. **The Blacker The Berry** (2015)
3. **Backseat Freestyle** (2012)
4. **King Kunta** (2015)
5. **Humble** (2017)
6. **Squabble Up** (2024)
7. **Bitch, Don't Kill My Vibe** (2012)
8. **DNA** (2017)
9. **Money Trees** (2012)
10. **Not Like Us** (2024)

The fans know when it's real. That's something that I always understood – just from being a fan myself.

Kendrick, on being real with his fans, interview with Lisa Robinson, *Vanity Fair*, June 28, 2018.

If my music were to stop today, how would I make my money stretch for the rest of my life? My kid's lifetime? My grandkids? If I stopped today, how would I do that? This could be my last moment and my last shot to keep that revenue coming. I got a lot of people to support… and a lot of people to inspire.

Kendrick, on money and supporting his family, interview with Insanula Ahmed, *Complex*, July 25, 2014.

I have to have at least 30 minutes to myself a day to just sit back, close my eyes, and absorb what's going on and the space that I'm in. I have to find a way to understand the space that I'm in and how I'm feeling at the moment. If I don't, time is going to zoom. That 30 minutes helps me to totally zone out and gives me a re-start, a refresh. It lets me know why I'm here, doing what I'm doing.

”

Kendrick, on his daily meditation routine, interview with Lisa Robinson, *Vanity Fair*, June 28, 2018.

I always thought it would be about the money, but what actually makes me happy is the fact that I can come up with something from scratch and then do it and then go to a place like London where I can hear people singing those exact words back to me – that's the ultimate high for me. There's nothing like it.

Kendrick, on what makes him happy, interview with Erykah Badu, *Interview*, April 23, 2013.

My musicality has been driving me since I was four years old, but it's how I execute it that's the ultimate challenge. Going from *To Pimp a Butterfly* to *DAMN.*, that shit could have crashed and burned if it wasn't executed right. So I had to be real careful on my subject matter and how I weave in and out of the topics so it still organically feels like me.

Kendrick, on his musicality and carefully selecting his lyrical material, interview with Brian Hiatt, *Rolling Stone*, August 9, 2017.

"

Can I outdo myself again? Can I make a better rhyme than I made last time? If that wasn't there, then I'd have stopped after I had my first platinum album. That's the challenge that keeps me going.

Kendrick, on the challenge of constantly trying to evolve as an artist, interview with Brian Hiatt, *Rolling Stone*, August 9, 2017.

I've never expressed myself the way I expressed myself on this album. From the moment I started picking up a pen and started freestyling, this was the moment in my life that I was trying to get to without even knowing at the time.

”

Kendrick, on his highly personal and acclaimed album 2022's *Mr. Morale & The Big Steppers*, interview with Mitchell S. Jackson, *New York Times*, December 27, 2022.

I saw Dr. Dre when I was nine years old in Compton – him and Tupac. They were shooting the second 'California Love' video. My pops had seen him and ran back to the house and put me on his shoulders, and we stood there watching Dre and Pac in a Bentley. I'll never forget this moment. The moment I met Dre, 15 years later, that moment was playing in my head…

When Dre was talking to me all I could think about was that moment when I was a kid. Right after that he told me 'Go in the booth,' I had to, in a split second, stop being a fan and get professional. That moment was make-or-break for me in my career, but I executed.

Kendrick, on the challenge of constantly trying to evolve as an artist, interview with Brian Hiatt, *Rolling Stone*, August 9, 2017.

Kendrick has many accolades to his name, from Billboard's 10 Best Rappers of All Time to People's Sexiest Man Alive, but it is his Grammy Awards which take pole position.

With 22 wins from 57 nominations, Kendrick is one of the most rewarded rappers in Grammy history – just three shy of Jay-Z's 25 wins.

His wins at the 67th annual ceremony in 2025 are perhaps the most special – Record of the Year and Song of the Year for 'Not Like Us'.

I've been writing my whole life, so to get this type of recognition – it's beautiful.

Kendrick, on his Pulitzer Prize in 2018.

Writing has given me the opportunity to learn about myself, find out who I am. When I'm writing, I've got to sit and go through the emotions and be vulnerable. It's for my own sanity.

”

Kendrick, on song writing for his sanity, interview with Timothée Chalamet, *Billboard*, February 7, 2025.

"

It was always the phrases that excited me the most about writing a rap. The wittiness, the clarity, how you manipulate words and make them mean other things. I practised the wording for a long time before I got the delivery down pat.

"

Kendrick, on his deep love of language and words as a child (despite being a stutterer*), interview with Dorian Lynskey, *The Guardian*, June 21, 2015.

* Rapping "on street corners" made Kendrick popular – and cured his stutter.

I was nurtured in an environment where there's lot of gang mentality. That certain language, certain lingo. How we walk. How we talk. All the little nuances and in-speaks that I have in Compton. I have that. That's not going nowhere. That's why I can go into any environment, and be able to still connect even at this high of a level. I'm the son that never leaves. That's nurture.

Kendrick, on being a son of Compton forever, interview with Mitchell S. Jackson, *New York Times*, December 27, 2022.

When you think of Compton, it's numb with negativity, even to this day. So the whole purpose of my first album was really to spark the idea of doing something different rather than doing a record that's just about gang culture. That's the ultimate thing I want to do in making music – to be able to inspire somebody else.

Kendrick, on positivity and gang culture, interview with Erykah Badu, *Interview*, April 23, 2013.

When I first started I spent more time listening to albums than writing songs. I think that gave me all the tricks in terms of wordplay, from how I pronounced my words to the actual delivery. I'm very intricate about that stuff when I go into the studio – the words in my raps have to sound the way I hear them in my head.

Kendrick, on perfecting his songwriting craft, interview with Erykah Badu, *Interview*, April 23, 2013.

I want you to get angry,
I want you to get happy.
I want you to feel disgusted.
I want you to feel
uncomfortable.

Kendrick, on the social and political themes on 2015's acclaimed album *To Pimp A Butterfly*, interview with Joe Coscarelli, *New York Times*, March 16, 2015.

When I really lock in, I lock in. I cut phones off for months. You can only reach me as long as you're my father, my mother, my sister, my brother. They know how to reach me but outside of that, the phone is off.

Kendrick, on his creative process when recording a new album, interview with Insanula Ahmed, *Complex*, July 25, 2014.

I'm a small guy – I only grew to 5ft 6in. I deferred my dreams to write in rhymes, and I pinned my dream [of being the next Michael Jordan] somewhere else.

Kendrick, on his stature and his former dreams of being a pro basketball player, interview with Brian Hiatt, *Rolling Stone*, August 9, 2017.

* Kendrick's height has helped: "Everybody was always bigger and older than me. But that gave me my own insight."

"

The Pulitzer Prize was one of those things I heard about in school, but I never thought I'd be a part of it. When I heard I got it, I thought, Whoa, this recognition by the academic world can take me above and beyond. But it's one of those things that should have happened with hip-hop a long time ago. For it to get the recognition that it deserves as a true art form, that's not only great for myself but hip-hop in general.

"

Kendrick, on the impact of the being the first rapper to win a prestigious Pulitzer Prize in 2018, interview with Lisa Robinson, *Vanity Fair*, June 28, 2018.

Everybody got their own journey but I was just fortunate enough to have a group of guys around me that gave me that courage to feed myself with the arts. I was always allowed to be myself.

”

Kendrick, on his family, friends and crew that encouraged him to flourish within the arts, interview with Mitchell S. Jackson, *New York Times*, December 27, 2022.

CHAPTER FOUR

BAD BLOOD

Got beef? Lamar is famed for his feuds with other rappers, as well as his Internet-breaking moments – of which there are a few – that prove he's not just the most influential artist of his generation but also a supremely entertaining one to boot.

To prove his point, Kendrick's fans – Kenfolk – use the name DRAKE as an acronym for Don't Rap Against Kendrick Ever.

Wise words, indeed...

Gotta go with Kendrick. I think Drake is an outstanding entertainer, but Kendrick, his lyrics – *To Pimp a Butterfly* was the best album of the year.

”

Barack Obama, on choosing a side between Kendrick and Drake, interview with Nick Robinson, *The Hill*, May 6, 2024.

I just wanted to give some advice to the young people out there, never get into a rap battle with Kendrick Lamar.

”

Sean Ono Lennon, at the Grammy Awards 2025, about Kendrick's Superbowl performance with Drake, as quoted in an interview with Stéphanie Binet, *Le Monde*, March 15, 2025.

Kendrick's infamous war of words with Canadian rapper Drake began in 2013 with Lamar's verse on Big Sean's 'Control'. From there, the feud spiralled into several bitter exchanges across many hit songs:

1. **Like That** – Kendrick's verse challenges Drake and J. Cole
2. **7 Minute Drill** – Released by J. Cole
3. **Push Ups** – Drake's direct response to Kendrick
4. **Taylor Made Freestyle** – Another track by Drake
5. **Euphoria** – Kendrick's rebuttal to Drake
6. **6:16 in LA** – Another response from Kendrick
7. **Family Matters** – Drake's counter to Kendrick's accusations
8. **Meet the Grahams** – Kendrick's diss track of Drake
9. **Not Like Us** – Kendrick is crowned King?

The beef has yet to be squashed...

I really wish I was best friends with Kendrick Lamar. And I'm not, and that makes me sad daily.

”

Taylor Swift, *Billboard*, January 2015.

It was the 2017 single 'Humble' that gave Kendrick his first solo No. 1 U.S. single. However, it was his renowned remix verse on Taylor Swift's 2015 worldwide smash 'Bad Blood', from her *1989* album, that made the pop world first pay attention to Kendrick's flow skills.

I have to make it count where fans truly understand: that's me pouring out my soul on a record. They're going to feel it because I too have pain. It might not be like mine, but they're going to feel it.

Kendrick, on connecting with his fans, interview with Joe Coscarelli, *New York Times*, March 16, 2015.

I like to help those who help themselves. Nothing's handed to you, that's how my pops taught me. I'm not into the self-pity at all. Get up off your ass and go do something... I sound like my pops right now!

Kendrick, on his own motto for life, interview with Insanula Ahmed, *Complex*, July 25, 2014.

“That’s some real beef.”

Kendrick, on the infamous Taylor Swift vs Katy Perry feud that was the subject matter of Swift’s 2014 hit ‘Bad Blood’, on which Kendrick contributed a killer remix verse in 2015, interview with Brian Hiatt, *Rolling Stone*, August 9, 2017.

The best entertainers have the most wickedest sense of humor, to be able to take pain and change it into laughter.

Kendrick, on the importance of humour in his music and performance, interview with Brian Hiatt, *Rolling Stone*, August 9, 2017.

The most fundamental aspect of telling a story is being able to tell one from start to finish, and making that puzzle come together at the end. That's the art for me.

”

Kendrick, on his acclaim as a one of rap's greatest storytellers, interview with Erykah Badu, *Interview*, April 23, 2013 .

Hip-hop plays two ways in my head: a contact sport, and also songwriting that you connect to. Growing up and listening to rap battles between Nas and Jay-Z, that's the sport for me. That's where it can get funky, that's where I can say whatever I want, however I want, whenever I want. Then there's the other side, which is showing something that people can actually relate to and connect with it. I have that competitive nature, and I also have the compassion to talk about something that's real.

Kendrick, on the two sides to hip-hop, interview with Kiana Fitzgerald, *Complex*, October 16, 2017.

Can you believe that we're both sitting in this Oval Office?

President Barack Obama

Kendrick was invited to the White House in January 2016 for a private meeting to discuss topics concerning the problems (and solutions) of inner city culture and embracing the youth, as well as the importance of mentorships for African-American children. "Sometimes I reflect to think back where would I be if I didn't have a presence of an older acquaintance telling me what's right and what's wrong," Lamar told the President.

For me to just jump into acting because I'm Kendrick Lamar, I'm not taking that pat on the back. I'll wait until I'm able to take some time off and study the craft.

”

Kendrick, on his desire one day to act in, and direct, a feature film, interview with Brian Hiatt, *Rolling Stone*, August 9, 2017.

To date, across his six studio albums, Kendrick has had five No. 1s on the U.S. Billboard 200 and has sold more than 70 million records in total.

This makes him one of the best-selling rappers of all time!

That's one thing that people don't understand – I'm not indulging in drugs because I just don't want to, I'm not doing it because I know me and I know my history and my family. Once I'm there, there's really no going back. That could be the demise of not only me, but the whole generation that's following me. That's a whole lot of responsibility.

Kendrick, on being drug and alcohol free, interview with Insanul Ahmed, *Complex*, July 25, 2014.

My favourite Drake song? I got a lot of favourite Drake songs. Can't name one off the back, but he has plenty.

Kendrick, on Drake, interview with Brian Hiatt, *Rolling Stone*, August 9, 2017.

“Hip-hop has always been the ultimate genre – it always moves the needle. We say what’s cool and what’s not cool. We tell you what it ain’t, if it ain’t it. We decide that. Simple as that. You can debate me on this all day you want.”

Kendrick, on hip-hop, interview with Zack O’Malley Greenburg, *Forbes*, November 14, 2017.

The minute I hear good news, it just motivates me to do more. I don't want to get complacent. If you asked seven out of ten people, 'What would you do if you got the Pulitzer prize?' they'd say, 'I'd put my feet up.' but that would make me feel I'd reached my pinnacle at 30 years old, and that wouldn't make me feel good.

99

Kendrick, on complacency and motivation, interview with Lisa Robinson, *Vanity Fair*, June 28, 2018.

Performing at the Super Bowl reminds me of the essence and the core response of rap and hip-hop – and how far it can go. It puts the culture on the forefront where it needs to be. And not minimized to a catchy song or verse. Rap is a true art form.

Kendrick, on being the first rapper to perform at the Super Bowl, Super Bowl Press Conference, *XXL Mag*, February 6, 2025.

I wrote most of my first album in my mom's kitchen, and now I can go around the world and hear people recite those lyrics, and understand my story, even though they're not from the same area I grew up in. I enjoy the fact that people aren't just listening to my music, but *hearing* it.

Kendrick, on the power of his songs, interview with Dave Chappelle, *Interview*, March 23, 2023.

I could have went. I should have went. It's always in the back of my mind. It's not too late.

”

Kendrick, on one day returning to college to finish his studies, interview with Marcus J. Moore, *The Nation*, October 8, 2020.

My music isn't for me; it's for people who are going through their struggles and want to relate to someone who feels the same way they do.

”

Kendrick, on relating to his fans, interview with Dave Chappelle, *Interview*, March 23, 2023.

My first grade teacher flipped out because I wrote the word 'audacity' in a story. She was like, 'Duckworth, I'll never forget that last name.' I never forgot that.

”

Kendrick, on his first grade teacher, Mr Inge, being impressed by his expansive vocabulary,* interview with Insanula Ahmed, *Complex*, July 25, 2014.

* "I only knew the word because I heard my auntie and uncles arguing and one would say, 'You got the audacity to take my motherfucking drink and pour it out!'"

I've been in that studio writing terrible verses, writing terrible hooks, with homeboys that you trust telling you, 'That's garbage.' I grew thick skin, got back in there and did it all over again. I learned how to challenge myself to take my raps to the next level.

Kendrick, on exceeding his limits, interview with Kiana Fitzgerald, *Complex*, October 16, 2017.

Execution is my favourite word. I spend 80 percent of my time thinking about how I'm going to execute my ideas, figuring out how I'm going to convey these words to a person to connect to it. My other favourite word is 'discipline'. Discipline gives me all my unvarnished strength and makes me curious about how disciplined I can be.

”

Kendrick, on his favourite words, interview with Lisa Robinson, *Vanity Fair*, Juno 28, 2018.

I got to write one line or idea down a day – I've got to do it.

Kendrick, on his songwriting process, interview with Insanula Ahmed, *Complex*, July 25, 2014.

“

To be someone with a good heart, and to still be harassed as a kid . . . it took a toll on me. Soon you're just saying, 'Fuck everything.' That line was me getting those frustrations out. And I'm glad I could get them out with a pen and a paper.

”

Kendrick, on the pen being mightier than the sword, interview with Marcus J. Moore, *The Nation*, October 8, 2020.

When I'm in the studio I'm looking for creativity I haven't matched yet. Not creativity that I've done and I know I can do 100,000 times. I'm looking for a feeling I haven't felt. It's a high, man. It's a drug.

Kendrick, on music as a drug, interview with Insanula Ahmed, *Complex*, July 25, 2014.

You could put all your feelings down on a sheet of paper, and they'd make sense to you? I liked that.

”

Kendrick, in seventh grade, learning about poetry, rhymes, metaphors and double-entendres from his English teacher Mr Inge, interview with Marcus J. Moore, *The Nation*, October 8, 2020.

CHAPTER FIVE

BLACK PANTHER

Kendrick's global super-stardom came with the release of 2015's *To Pimp A Butterfly*, an album that showcased his raw and rare talents and led to him curating the now-iconic Black Panther soundtrack album in 2018.

Now at his creative peak, this is Kendrick on his rise to become rap's most-influential role model, the struggle of the black community, his fans, and the constant fight to battle the pressures of fame and fortune...

Kendrick and Black Panther – it was a perfect marriage.

Ryan Coogler, director of *Black Panther*, NPR, February 2018.

In 2018, Kendrick curated a 14-song soundtrack to *Black Panther*, the first Marvel movie of the original black superhero, to accompany the original score. For the album, Kendrick wrote and performed on 10 tracks and collaborated with a feast of American rap talent, all chosen by him, including SZA, the Weekend, Travis Scott and Anderson Paak.

Lamar's role as producer and curator of the *Black Panther* soundtrack showcased his ability to merge music with cinema. The soundtrack became a cultural phenomenon in its own right, complementing the themes of the Marvel blockbuster while continuing Lamar's legacy of producing impactful, socially conscious art.

"When I was just hanging out and somebody drives by, starts shooting, and the bullet barely misses me but it hits my homey and kills him, I'm back to reality. Those were the days I felt I was never going to make it as a rapper."

Kendrick, when asked "Did you ever think you'd make it as a successful rapper?", interview with Dorian Lynskey, *The Guardian*, June 21, 2015.

I had to be right there from the trenches in order for fans to believe me. My track record can back it up… That's why people are able to connect with me… I embrace everything that I've ever been through. I just try to convey it and hopefully the people can understand it.

Kendrick, on not glorifying his past, interview with Insanula Ahmed, *Complex*, July 25, 2014.

"When we don't have respect for ourselves, how do we expect them to respect us?"

Kendrick, on Black lives and pride in America, interview with Joe Coscarelli, *New York Times*, March 16, 2015.

I've been to too many funerals. Ever since I was little, I've wondered why it doesn't stop.

Kendrick, on the constant gang shootings of his homeboys in the Compton hood, interview with Stéphanie Binet, *Le Monde*, March 15, 2025.

I remember riding with my pops down the street and looking out the window and seeing motherfuckers just running. I can see smoke. We stop, and my pops goes into the Auto-Zone and comes out rolling four tires. I know he didn't buy them.

Kendrick, on April 29, 1992, the first day of the notorious South Central LA riots and the looting aftermath, interview with Marcus J. Moore, *The Nation*, October 8, 2020.

“I could be both.”

Kendrick, when asked, "Are you a pimp or a butterfly?", interview with Marcus J. Moore, *The Nation*, October 8, 2020.

I remember when *Good Kid* came out, the people I grew up with literally cried tears of joy when they listened to it – because these are people who have been shunned out of society. And for me to tell my story, which is their story as well, they felt that someone saw them as more than just killers or drug dealers.

”

Kendrick, on the impact of his second album and first major success, interview with Lisa Robinson, *Vanity Fair*, June 28, 2018.

In March 2026 Kendrick will feature as an actor in the movie *Whitney Springs*, directed by Trey Parker, the co-creator of South Park. Parker first met Kendrick in 2022 for the song 'The Heart Part 5', which employed deepfake technology created by Parker's studio, Deep Voodoo.

Whitney Springs tells the story of a "young black man [Lamar] who, while interning as a slave reenactor at a living history museum, discovers that his white girlfriend's ancestors once owned his". The movie has been labelled a "slave comedy musical" and promises to be unlike any film ever made.

The police – the biggest gang in California. You'll never win against them.

Kendrick, on the LAPD, after his friend was murdered by a police officer in 2007, interview with Marcus J. Moore, *The Nation*, October 8, 2020.

It was mayhem in LA. I said to my mom, 'So the police beat up a black man, and now everybody's mad? OK. I get it now.'

”

Kendrick, on the brutal police death of Rodney King in 1992 and the notorious South Central LA riots that followed, when Kendrick was aged five, interview with Marcus J. Moore, *The Nation*, October 8, 2020.

I've hurt people in my life. It's something I still have to think about when I sleep at night. I don't talk about these things if I haven't lived them.

”

Kendrick, on mistakes he's made, interview with Marcus J. Moore, *The Nation*, October 8, 2020.

Under the Influence

The 10 albums that made Kendrick Lamar into the greatest rapper of his generation. It all started here:

1. ***Quik Is The Name*** (1991) – DJ Quik
2. ***Death Certificate*** (1991) – Ice Cube
3. ***The Chronic*** (1992) – Dr. Dre
4. ***Doggystyle*** (1993) – Snoop Dogg
5. ***Ready To Die*** (1994) – Notorious B.I.G.
6. ***Me Against The World*** (1995) – 2Pac
7. ***Dogg Food*** (1995) – Tha Dogg Pound
8. ***Reasonable Doubt*** (1996) – Jay-Z
9. ***It's Dark and Hell is Hot*** (1998) – DMX
10. ***The Block Is Hot*** (1999) – Lil Wayne

What gives me inspiration is giving inspiration to people who don't have it – I'm putting in the real work with street kids and ex-convicts.

Kendrick, on giving back to the community that raised him through funding and donating to local mentorship programs and rehabilitation charities, interview with Joe Coscarelli, *New York Times*, March 16, 2015.

My [oldest and closest friends from Compton] have 10, 15, 20 years left in prison, but I can go into prison – and I do – and tell them that when they get out, they have a job. And my word stands.

”

Kendrick, on helping out his incarcerated friends from Compton, interview with Lisa Robinson, *Vanity Fair*, June 28, 2018.

I've been on this earth for 30 years, and there's been so many things a Caucasian person said I couldn't do. Get good credit. Buy a house in an urban city. So many things – 'you can't do that' – whether it's from afar or close up. So if I say this is my word, let me have this one word, please let me have that word.

Kendrick, on white people not being allowed to say the N-word, interview with Lisa Robinson, *Vanity Fair*, June 28, 2018.

"

Whenever I wasn't on the streets with my homeys, I was in the studio. It was something that kept me out of trouble. So my mom would let me stay out till four in the morning because she knew I was doing that.

"

Kendrick, on music as salvation from the streets, interview with Dorian Lynskey, *The Guardian*, June 21, 2015.

When people ask for my rider, they think I'm crazy: Fruity Pebbles, baked chicken, bottle of Hennessy and some Polo socks. My grandma always told me, 'You ain't got to take a shower for four days, but put some fresh socks on and you'll feel better about yourself.'

”

Kendrick, on his less-than-demanding backstage tour rider – and his love of breakfast cereals and socks, interview with Erykah Badu, *Interview*, April 23, 2013.

I went to South Africa – Durban, Cape Town, Johannesburg – and those were definitely the 'I've arrived' shows. Outside of the money, the success, the accolades, this is a place that we, in urban communities, never dream of – this is the motherland. I felt it as soon as I touched down. Being there changed my whole perspective on how to convey my art.

Kendrick, on his unforgettable trip to South Africa in 2014, and how visiting Robben Island and other historical sites significantly influenced his album *To Pimp a Butterfly* by inspiring him to create music that reflected a broader perspective on the Black experience and his sense of belonging in Africa, interview with Dave Chappelle, *Interview*, March 23, 2023.

When I look at how society has shaped our communities, it's been generations passed down of putting people in cages to battle each other.

”

Kendrick, on the centuries-long struggle of Black America, interview with Lisa Robinson, *Vanity Fair*, June 28, 2018.

I've had rewards for my other albums in different ways, whether it was accolades, whether it was the Pulitzer, whether it was the Grammys. For *Mr Morale*, the reward for me was humanity. I thought about my children. I thought about when they turn 21, or they're older in life, and I'm long gone – this album can be a prerequisite of how to cope.

”

Kendrick, on 2022's "uncompromising honesty" as reward for *Mr Morale and The Big Steppers*, interview with Briana Younger, *W Magazine*, October 11, 2022.

> “We lost a lot of homies to some street shit, and for all of us to be on this stage together, unity from each side of mother-fucking LA, Crips, Bloods, Pirus, this shit is special, man.”

Kendrick, on his one-off unity concert The Pop Out: Ken & Friends at the Kia Forum in Inglewood, California, to showcase how the West Coast rap scene is bigger than its tragedies, June 19, 2024.

For what I do, there is certainly no growth without vulnerability – vulnerability is not a weakness.

Kendrick, on allowing himself to be vulnerable for his music, interview with SZA, *Harper's Bazaar*, October 21, 2024.

I remember the first time I actually understood gangbanging, I was in kindergarten. We was having a house party and my uncle – who was in the Compton Crips – was like 'Cuz' this and 'Cuz' that and, 'Yeah, cuz. I had the blue thing on.' I'm like, 'What is cuz? Why does he keep saying blue?' The next week, when I went back to school there was an older kid who was like, 'You know what a Crip and Blood is?' and I was like, 'Yeah, a Crip is blue and a Blood is red.'

Kendrick, on first learning about Compton gang life, interview with Insanula Ahmed, *Complex*, July 25, 2014.

My mom always told me: 'How long you going to play the victim?' I can say I'm mad and I hate everything, but nothing really changes until I change myself. So no matter how much bullshit we've been through as a community, I'm strong enough to say fuck that and acknowledge myself and my own struggles

Kendrick, on focusing on his own personal growth as a means to change his situation, interview with Marcus J. Moore, *The Nation*, October 8, 2020.

I've had a few years of success and celebrity, but I can't get rid of the 20 years of being with my homies. I can't throw that away. I know a lot of people who could –I've seen it – be like, 'Fuck you. I've got money now, I'm outta here. I don't give a fuck about none of y'all.' But that was something I couldn't deal with. I had to sit back and figure out other ways I could impact these people without physically trying to bring the whole hood inside a hotel.

”

Kendrick, on remembering his roots after the fame and fortune, interview with Lisa Robinson, *Vanity Fair*, June 28, 2018.

If you come from a negative place and you're doing something positive, that's change within itself. Sometimes you'll go so far that the people that you used to be with can't relate. All you can try to do is help them and share some of the gains and knowledge.

Kendrick, on using his fame for personal growth, interview with Insanula Ahmed, *Complex*, July 25, 2014.

CHAPTER SIX

NOT LIKE US

Kendrick Lamar is not like the rest of us.

Here, in his own words, he tells us the reasons and his life philosophies behind why he's the GOAT, the real deal, and the most inspiring rapper of his generation. Pay attention…

I know I have a purpose. God put something in my heart to get across and that's using my voice as an instrument, and doing what needs to be done, not just for myself or my generation, but even a higher cause than that. When it's said and done, I'll be able to talk about it.

”

Kendrick, on using his voice for good and God, interview with Insanula Ahmed, *Complex*, July 25, 2014.

Always do something that you feel good about. Don't do something because you want to get signed or you want a distribution deal – that doesn't last. What lasts is something that is 100 per cent true to yourself. Some artists get so twisted and tangled in the hit singles and how many streams other artists get that they lose vision of the creative process. My biggest mistake was watching the other artists' success and thinking that can be my own success.

Kendrick, on his advice for aspiring artists and rappers, interview with Zack O'Malley Greenburg, *Forbes*, November 14, 2017.

Failure is the one thing that stops us all from being our own entrepreneurs and following our own dreams, and having ownership in what we do, because we're scared of what people are going to think, we're scared about the money we're going to lose. Your failures and mistakes may be on you, right here and right now, but at the end of the day these are lessons learned.

Kendrick, on not fearing failure, interview with Zack O'Malley Greenburg, *Forbes*, November 14, 2017.

I can't change the world until I change myself first. If you made my family hurt, I want to hurt yours. Them emotions still run in me. Whether I'm a rap star or not, if I still feel like that, then I'm part of the problem rather than the solution.

Kendrick, on his desire to grow as a person, interview with Marcus J. Moore, *The Nation*, October 8, 2020.

I know that from being on tour – kids are living by my music. I'm the closest thing to a preacher that they have. But my word will never be as strong as God's word. All I am is just a vessel, doing his work.

Kendrick, on God's input with his music, interview with *Relevant Magazine*, March 16, 2015.

If I can make one person – or 10 million people – feel a certain type of euphoria in my music, that's the whole point.

”

Kendrick, on the power and purpose of his music, interview with Brian Hiatt, *Rolling Stone*, August 9, 2017.

> Nobody can tell my story the way I tell it.

Kendrick, on his uniqueness, interview with Brian Hiatt, *Rolling Stone*, August 9, 2017.

I'm human. I make mistakes just like you. I'll probably make the same mistake you made yesterday, today for myself.

Kendrick, on being human, interview with Insanula Ahmed, *Complex*, July 25, 2014.

I feel my work in music is just the start. I don't think it's my end goal. I know it's not my end goal. Music is just a vessel to get me there.

Kendrick, on life after music, interview with SZA, *Harper's Bazaar*, October 21, 2024.

In this lifestyle, everything is at your reach, whatever you want, whatever you need. When those cameras are on you, you can get anything you need. But who you really are is when the lights cut off and all you have left is your discipline.

”

Kendrick, on discipline and temptation, interview with Brian Hiatt, *Rolling Stone*, August 9, 2017.

"

'Not Like Us' is the energy of who I am, the type of man I represent. Now, if you identify with the man that I represent… This man has morals, he has values, he believes in something, he stands for something. He's not pandering. He's a man who can recognize his mistakes and not be afraid to share the mistakes and can dig deep down into fear-based ideologies or experiences to be able to express them without feeling like he's less of a man.

"

Kendrick, on 'Not Like Us' and the power it represents, interview with SZA, *Harper's Bazaar*, October 21, 2024.

I like to be alone a lot. I need that. It's that duality: I can go in front of a crowd of 100,000 people and express myself, then go back, be alone, and collect my thoughts all over again.

”

Kendrick, on protecting his mental health, interview with Lisa Robinson, *Vanity Fair*, June 28, 2018.

Man, I was so excited! I didn't know what to do with it. To tell you the truth I wanted to spend it as fast as I could on whatever I dreamed about. The kid in me, the person who never had nothing growing up, is saying, 'I want to spend this shit on some chains and a car!'

Kendrick, on what he did when he got his first big pay check, interview with Dorian Lynskey, *The Guardian*, June 21, 2015.

"

A lot of artists have a fear of success, they can't handle it; some people need drugs to escape. For me, I need the microphone – that's how I release it.

"

Kendrick, on how he handles his fame, interview with Lisa Robinson, *Vanity Fair*, June 28, 2018.

Everything that we glorified in the hood – smoking, drinking, women, violence – was at my feet times 10. All of it's there. With success comes power. That is temptation at its highest.

”

Kendrick, on his first taste of fame, interview with Dorian Lynskey, *The Guardian*, June 21, 2015.

This fame shit don't happen to everybody. Almost all of my best friends are in prison. Forty years plus.

”

Kendrick, on making it (and his friends not), interview with Brian Hiatt, *Rolling Stone*, August 9, 2017.

"

I'm always locked in, and I'm always trying new things – whether or not I like them is a whole other conversation. But I have to keep the pen warm. That's probably one of the biggest misconceptions about me as an artist.

"

Kendrick, on the "biggest misconception" about him as an artist – his love of experimentation, interview with Timothée Chalamet, *Billboard*, February 7, 2025.

“

I’m the first in my family to have this kind of success, so I took it upon myself to wisely navigate this success, because I wanted them to be successful too.

”

Kendrick, on success, interview with Lisa Robinson, *Vanity Fair*, June 28, 2018.

I know the reason why I'm so good: because God's blessed me with the talent to execute on the talent. But I can easily smell my own bullshit – the moment that you start getting lost in your ego, that's when you start going down.

Kendrick, on why he's the "greatest rapper alive" and his ego, interview with Mitchell S. Jackson, *New York Times*, December 27, 2022.

To a lot of people I knew growing up, the glass was always halfway empty. You got to be a muthafuckin' optimist to make it that's for sure. And it's not just being optimistic. It's really about being responsible. You can talk about dreams all day but you got to put an action behind it too.

Kendrick, on being a proactive optimist, Brian Hiatt, *Rolling Stone*, August 9, 2017.

At first, all I knew was masculinity and bravado – and I always kept that wall up because of my pops. But the more I delve deeper into my music and the more expressive I get with myself... that is the feminine energy right there. This is who I am, the soft-spoken me, and I have to own it. This is where my superpower lies.

Kendrick, on his reputation as being gentle and softly-spoken, interview with SZA, *Harper's Bazaar*, October 21, 2024.

"

What makes a hit record? Is it the amount of streams or sales or spins on the radio? Nobody can really justify it. I've heard hundreds of records from inside the neighbourhood that were quote-unquote 'hit records' but never stood a chance outside the community.

"

Kendrick, on the quality of the raps he heard on street corners that were never made into successful songs, interview with Andrew Barker, *Variety*, November 21, 2017.

I have so much discipline as far as repetition – I don't give a fuck if it's a thousand push-ups or pull-ups, I always give that extra five percent and ask myself, 'What's going to be the evolution for myself today?' That's what keeps me creative… I'm not even the same person as I was yesterday.

”

Kendrick, on avoiding repeating himself, interview with Brian Younger, *W Magazine*, October 11, 2022.

You can't change where you from. You can't take a person out of their zone and expect them to be somebody else now that they in the record industry. It's going to take years. Years of travelling. Years of meeting people. Years of seeing the world.

”

Kendrick, on his journey of personal growth, interview with Jessica Hopper, *Spin*, October 9, 2012.

I'm not an angry person. But I do believe in love and war – and I believe both need to exist.

Kendrick, on war and peace, interview with SZA, *Harper's Bazaar*, October 21, 2024.

In my early years, I was all just about the raps. I didn't care about nothing else. But when you get into the world of songwriting, and making material that's universal, and I had to be hands on and learn the different sounds and frequencies, and what makes people move, what melodies stick, taking the higher octaves and the lower octaves and learning how to intertwine that in a certain frequency. Basically, how to manipulate sound to your advantage.

Kendrick, on expanding his musical knowledge and vocabulary with each new album, interview with Andrew Barker, *Variety*, November 21, 2017.

I literally talk to God. Like, it's to a point where I'll be starting to think I'm going crazy. But then He has to remind me, 'No, this is really me'.

Kendrick, on his relationship with God, interview with SZA, *Harper's Bazaar*, October 21, 2024.

I've grown as an artist. I've learned that my mission statement is really self-expression. I don't want anybody to classify my music. I want people to say, 'This is somebody who's recognizing his true feelings, his true emotions, ideas, thoughts, opinions and views on the world, all on one record.' I want people to recognize that and to take it and apply it to their own lives.

Kendrick, on the values he hopes fans hear in his music, interview with Dave Chappelle, *Interview*, March 23, 2023.

I love being present. Being in the now and just being locked in to how I feel and the energy I have now is something that I will carry into New Orleans for the world to see... I want that energy to ooze out the television and the people in that stadium.

Kendrick, on what he hopes fans will enjoy about his now-iconic Super Bowl halftime performance, Super Bowl press conference, *XXL Mag*, February 6, 2025.

February 9, 2025

The day Kendrick Lamar made history. He headlined the Super Bowl halftime show during Super Bowl LIX at Caesars Superdome in New Orleans – the first solo hip-hop artist to do so in the history of the sport.

His 13-minute set struck a chord with the 80,000-strong crowd and featured a mix of his greatest hits, including 'Humble', 'DNA' and 'Euphoria'.

Of course, the standout moment was his diss-track 'Not Like Us', a performance that reignited his infamous beef with fellow rapper, Drake. The moment went viral and is now considered a major milestone not just in Kendrick's career but popular culture.

Here's the thing about gangbanging. I was born in Compton – you have to be affiliated. Gangs is my family, I grew up with them, I hung with them. So, I been around it, been through it, but I can't sit here and claim a gang.

”

Kendrick, on his reputation as being gang-affiliated, interview with Jessica Hopper, *Spin*, October 9, 2012.

"

I want to meet people smarter than me. I want to talk to them. I want them to show me things. I just want to be fulfilled with whatever this world has to offer. That shit hypes me up. *Information.* I'm a motherfucking nerd for it.

"

Kendrick, on knowledge and his desire for it, interview with SZA, *Harper's Bazaar*, October 21, 2024.

How do I handle fans? The simplest way I can. What would I rather be doing? Would I rather be on the corner running from bullets all day or would I rather be taking pictures? What shot do I want? A shot from a nine-millimetre or an iPhone shot with a fan? Once I remember that… I realise I'm blessed, man.

Kendrick, on interacting with his fans, interview with Dorian Lynskey, *The Guardian*, June 21, 2015.